# Proclaim Jesus Workbook

# Proclaim Jesus Workbook

## Learn How to Easily Share Your Faith with Friends

Women Inseparable Workbook

Jaclyn Palmer
Inseparable Ministries Publishing
Meridian, Idaho, 2023

Proclaim Jesus Workbook: Learn How to Easily Share Your
Faith with Friends

Copyright © 2023 by Jaclyn Palmer

First Printing 2023

ISBN 979-8-9879788-2-5

Cover design by Linda Boatman
Edited by Kelly Murray
Published in the United States of America

Inseparable Ministries Publishing
1200 N Main Street
Meridian, Idaho
www.womeninseparable.com

# Scripture

How then will they call on him
in whom they have not believed?
And how are they to believe in him
of whom they have never heard?
And how are they to hear
without someone preaching?
And how are they to preach
unless they are sent?
As it is written,
"How beautiful are the feet
of those who preach the good news!"
Romans 10:14–15

How beautiful upon the mountains
are the feet of him who brings good news,
who publishes peace,
who brings good news of happiness,
who publishes salvation,
who says to Zion, "Your God reigns."
Isaiah 52:7

# Table of Contents

# Introduction to This Study

In the Proclaim Jesus Workbook, you will find yourself being with Jesus in four beautiful places: At the Cross, Before the Throne, On the Rock, and In His Presence. Here is what is included in each place:

- a short reading
- thoughts to ponder
- notes pages to use or not (this is your book—no rules)
- homework sections to complete with Jesus

Coordinating Proclaim Jesus **video teachings** are available for each place. Whether you are doing this workbook alone, with friends, or in a workshop, it is beneficial to watch the video before each place study. Videos can be found at:
womeninseparable.com/proclaim-jesus

If you are participating in a Proclaim Jesus Workshop, you will have the opportunity to complete the homework with those around you. If we can assist you in offering a Proclaim Jesus Workshop to the women of your church or ministry, please contact us at:
inseparableministriesinc@gmail.com

## A personal note...

What does the name of Jesus Christ feel like on your heart? What does it feel like within your mind, your thoughts? Furthermore, what does the name of Jesus feel like on your tongue?

Have you ever pondered His name and its impact within every part of your life? My prayer is that you will fall in love with the name of Jesus. As a child of God, you are saved and made new—daily—through the life and the blood of God's Son, Jesus Christ. Yet, there are moments in our daily lives when we forget to bring in our very Savior. Ponder that particular part of your living. Do you see His absence there? Consider that He is not absent there, for He has said, *"I will never leave you nor forsake you"* (Hebrews 13:5 ESV). So, where that feeling of absence resides there is a personal responsibility that arises. That responsibility and, if I may say, personal challenge sits in your hands. You can fill that absence through your expression of the very name of Jesus.

How do we proclaim the name of Jesus? This is the question that we will focus on as we are, where we are. For each of us are in different places in this question.

My request is that we walk together through each place found in this quest. May we stand together in the proclamation of the sweetest of all names. If we find ourselves further than those around us, may we become a listening ear and an encouragement to the one practicing their place. If those around us are further than we are, may we turn our thoughts to that of gleaning from their experiences rather than the thoughts of comparison that will only lead to self-condemnation.

As at all Women Inseparable events, there are no rules or expectations in this workshop. There is, however, homework. The homework centers around you and Jesus. I highly encourage you not to pursue and process through this workshop without Jesus. Take your time in the first step of this adventure, for the first step will make or break the rest of the journey.

Thank you for joining us as Women Inseparable. Thank you, deeper still, for proclaiming the name of Jesus Christ!

1 Corinthians 15:3–4,

*Jaclyn Palmer*

# *Place One* - At the Cross

## How do I proclaim the name of Jesus?

Place one begins where all things begin. It begins at the cross. At the cross, Jesus suffered the separation from God the Father on your behalf. Sit with that sentence, with that truth.

Jesus suffered the feeling of separation from God—physically, mentally, emotionally, and spiritually.

What did that feel like for Jesus?

# Notes/Journal

Take some time to write down your thoughts and questions.
Write down Scriptures, what you've learned, and what you want
to learn more about.

Being separated from God is part of humanity, due to the seed of evil that was birthed and planted within all mankind that dreadful day in history in the Garden of Eden, between one man and his wife. That one moment brought forth a separation from God.

What did these first experiences of separation feel like? Both Adam and Eve knew what being inseparable felt like. And then they knew what being separated from God felt like. Cain and Abel were born in separation from God. Cain felt that separation. Abel felt that separation. If you spent time with one of them, what would their story sound like? Will you pick one and sit with him or her this week? Intently listen to the heart of their experience.

Which of these four did you sit with? What passages did you meditate on? What did the heart of their story sound like in your heart?

It was at this very point in which God's love for the world began to thread the name of Jesus throughout generations to breach this eternal separation. God's love that gave His one and only Son would heal man's internal emptiness. And it would repair man back to being created in God's likeness. God's plan involved Jesus—in every way.

Jesus was submissive to God's plan.

# Notes/Journal

Take some time to write down your thoughts and questions.
Write down Scriptures, what you've learned, and what you want
to learn more about.

The seed of evil was plucked up and destroyed that beautifully painful day on the hill called Golgotha between one Man and His Father. That one moment brought forth a separation from God. Jesus felt that separation. God felt that separation. Creation itself felt that separation. Religion felt that separation. What did this separation look like? What did it feel like for Jesus? Spend time in Matthew 27. Listen to the sounds of separation expressed throughout this chapter. What sounds do you hear? What do these sounds feel like in your heart?

Today is about you. In light of the separation felt throughout time between the created and the Creator, what did your separation feel like? As part of humanity, you were born separated from God. Do you remember that separation? How can you describe that feeling in one word?

On the most beautiful day in history, Jesus Christ rose from the dead. The seed of evil was conquered and man's separation from God was restored. Jesus and God were together in full restoration. The created and the Creator were now gifted with an eternal relationship. Jesus won and continuously sings His song of victory over sin and death. Jesus extends His love, His life and blood, His forgiveness and freedom to all who submit to God's plan of salvation.

# Notes/Journal

Take some time to write down your thoughts and questions.
Write down Scriptures, what you've learned, and what you want
to learn more about.

Today is about you and Jesus. What did it feel like to receive God's gift of salvation? Can you describe what receiving that gift felt like or looked like?

In the light of God's love for the world, for you, what did Jesus give you when you received His gift of eternal life? How can you describe that truth in one word?

Sweet friend, do you see Jesus's story in you? It is in this story in which you stand. It is Jesus in you that you proclaim. It is this Way, this Truth, this Life that will walk with you in this workshop and throughout your life, your days, your moments, your conversations, and your proclamation of the name of Jesus.

# Notes/Journal

Take some time to write down your thoughts and questions. Write down Scriptures, what you've learned, and what you want to learn more about.

# Homework

Form Jesus's story in you in one sentence. Some of us may need to work out the words to center it on the seed of faith that saved us. To do this, practice removing words such as *church*, *religion*, *a person's name*, *a particular situation*. The only names in your sentence are your name and Jesus's. Take time with this assignment. Talk it out with the Lord and with those in your group.

Some of us may need to work this out in our hearts. You may be sitting here unable to formulate your sentence because your story has always been about church or religion or habit or _____.

Friend, you may be sitting here with the realization that you have never received Jesus as your personal Lord and Savior. You are in a good place. For without this realization, you will never be able to proclaim the name of Jesus to others with a comfortable understanding of Who He is. We must individually proclaim the name of Jesus to Jesus first. We must call upon His name, declaring our need for Him.

My question for you is this: Do you want to receive Jesus as your Savior today? I pray you will say *yes*. Not to me or to those around you but to Jesus.

# Homework

*But what does it say?*
*"The word is near you,*
*in your mouth and in your heart"*
*(that is, the word of faith that we proclaim);*
*because, if you confess with your mouth*
*that Jesus is Lord*
*and believe in your heart*
*that God raised him from the dead,*
*you will be saved.*
*For the Scripture says,*
*"Everyone who believes in him*
*will not be put to shame."*
*For there is no distinction between Jew and Greek;*
*for the same Lord is Lord of all,*
*bestowing his riches on all who call on him.*
*For "everyone who calls on the name of the Lord*
*will be saved."*
**Romans 10:8–9, 11–13**

Will you call upon the name of the Lord Jesus Christ today?

# Homework

First, jot down some key words from your salvation story. Then, look over all your words and pick out only three words: Jesus, you, and the one thing Jesus did for your heart. Finally, write your three words into a simple yet personal Salvation Sentence.

## Key Words

_____

_____

_____

_____

_____

_____

( 1 )  Jesus

( 2 )  Me

( 3 )  _____

## My Salvation Sentence

_____

_____

# Memory Goal

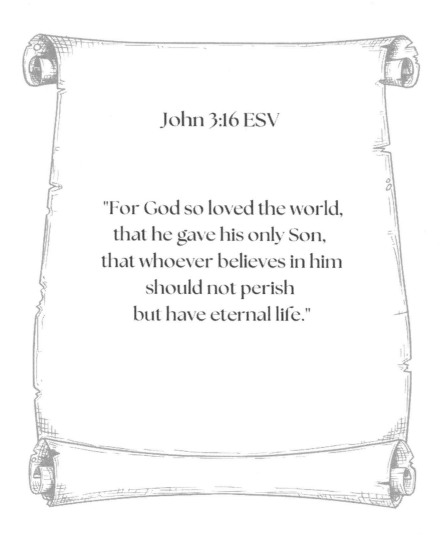

John 3:16 ESV

"For God so loved the world,
that he gave his only Son,
that whoever believes in him
should not perish
but have eternal life."

# *Place Two* - Before the Throne

## With whom do I proclaim the name of Jesus?

*"Let us therefore strive to enter that rest, so that no one may fall by the same sort of disobedience"* (Hebrews 4:11 ESV). This verse is an extensive historical reminder of the word *rest*. In the Old Testament, the Israelites lost sight of the promised rest by setting their gaze and their actions on this world.

Hebrews opens the door for New Testament believers to experience the same rest God offered to those of the Old Testament. This rest is eternal. It is today.

# Notes/Journal

Take some time to write down your thoughts and questions. Write down Scriptures, what you've learned, and what you want to learn more about.

As a child of God, to enter and reside in this rest is our promise of eternal life, today. We find this rest before the Throne.

May we crave that rest, together!

Peter reminds us in his second letter how vital it is to cling to the forgiveness of our sins. For, he says, the one who forgets has lost his sight altogether.

I declare that today, as we strive for our promised rest, that we do so in declaration of the forgiveness of our sins, within the ears and the hearts of those who surround us before the Throne of our Almighty God.

We are invited always and at all times to come to the Throne of God. Pause and consider the intimacy of this forever gift from God to us. Selah.

In our invitation we are encouraged to accept our place before the Throne with boldness. My question for us in our Proclaim Jesus Workshop is, What does that invitation with boldness look like? Furthermore, what does that sound like?

Truly, sketch this image in your head. You can do so by listing all that your senses are taking in as you visualize your place before the Throne. Utilize your five senses. Clearly, our vision will be through our flesh and the inability to fully know as stated in 1 Corinthians 13. But we are called forward in boldness in our flesh.

# Notes/Journal

Take some time to write down your thoughts and questions.
Write down Scriptures, what you've learned, and what you want
to learn more about.

So, we must in our flesh attempt to grasp the fullness of what this looks like, today. Spend time with God as you consider these things:

- What do you see before you? Around you?

- Who do you know on earth that you see beside you before the Throne?

- What words do you hear being expressed from hearts to His heart?

- Which of these words are yours?

- Which of these words do you hear pouring out from your friends? Your "enemies"?

Hebrews 4:14–16 gives us such beautiful imagery. May we use these verses to strengthen our confession of who our God is on a deeply personal level. And may we share the words that we find before the Throne with those who we know are kneeling beside us. Glorify God together through your testimony of all He is, all He has done in your life, and all that you sit in awe of before the Throne. May we have these conversations with boldness and love for God and for one another.

Oh, that we may know how to magnify God for the mighty act of eternal life through the forgiveness of our sins because of the gracious love of His Son and our Savior, Jesus Christ!

# Notes/Journal

Take some time to write down your thoughts and questions.
Write down Scriptures, what you've learned, and what you want
to learn more about.

# Homework

Share Jesus's story in you with those who know Jesus's story in them. What a beautiful conversation to have in the safety of the Throne Room! Find your words, your tone, your confidence as you practice sharing your Salvation Sentence with a trusted child of God.

As you engage in conversation, here are a few personal challenges:

- Begin with sharing your Salvation Sentence—nothing more. Simply that one sentence from Place One: Jesus and you.

- From there, receive/request one question from your friend. As you ponder that question, find a way to answer it by pointing it back to your Salvation Sentence. Do this exercise each time you engage in conversation before the Throne. You will notice how vast your story is and how applicable every detail of your story is to various hearts in various seasons.

Life lesson to put in your back pocket—not all people need all your life story all at one time. God knows what each heart needs from your life at that exact moment. Practice answering questions in simple ways, always pointing that answer back to your Salvation Sentence.

# Homework

**My Salvation Sentence:**

**Step One:** Consider who is beside you before the Throne.

**Step Two:** Share Jesus's story in you with that person on your heart.

**Step Three:** Repeat steps one and two, always. :)

**Step Four:** Report out in the Proclaim Jesus Workshop.

# Homework

## Pieces of My Story

If it's helpful, use this form to track the pieces of your story the Spirit has used.

Process (call, text, in person, email)
Location (work, church, coffee, etc...)
Outcome (What happened? Any next steps?)

| Name | Date | Process | Location | Outcome |
|------|------|---------|----------|---------|
|      |      |         |          |         |
|      |      |         |          |         |
|      |      |         |          |         |

# Homework

## My Vision at the Throne

What do you see before the Throne? What do you hear? What do you feel? Describe your senses here.

# Memory Goal

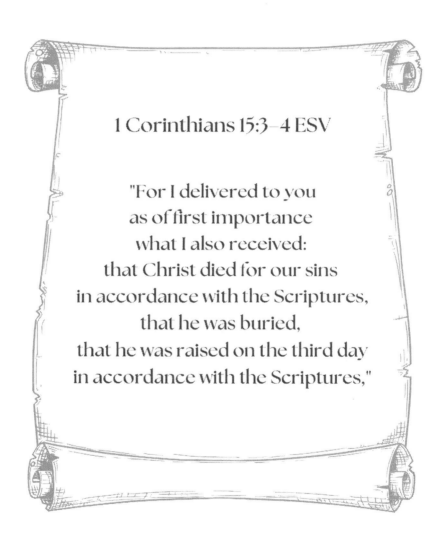

1 Corinthians 15:3–4 ESV

"For I delivered to you
as of first importance
what I also received:
that Christ died for our sins
in accordance with the Scriptures,
that he was buried,
that he was raised on the third day
in accordance with the Scriptures,"

# *Place Three* - On the Rock

## How do I know if they know the name of Jesus?

Do you see the ground beneath your feet? Allow this question to go with you throughout the week. No matter where you are or what you are doing, visualize the ground, the Rock, on which you stand.

You will always be on that Rock. Always. Whether it's Monday or Thursday, whether you are at work or at the store, whether you are in a pleasant mood or having a day, the Rock never moves. Therefore, your place on the Rock is secure.

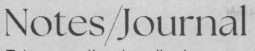

# Notes/Journal

Take some time to write down your thoughts and questions.
Write down Scriptures, what you've learned, and what you want
to learn more about.

With the visual of you on the Rock, visualize each person you come in contact with throughout the day and ask yourself, Are they on the Rock or are they not? It is one or the other. It cannot be both.

There are two ways of knowing whether they are on the Rock or not on the Rock, whether they have a relationship with Jesus Christ or they do not have a relationship with God through Jesus Christ.

- By their fruits

- By asking them

I propose that during our time in this workshop we remove number one and focus on number two. May we not assume who is on the Rock and who is not. What a wonderful way to engage in natural conversation with others.

How can you naturally ask another person about their knowledge of Jesus? This will be our intentional focus this week. Here's where the challenge comes in—there is no way of creating a "You Are Here" map.

Every person and every encounter is special and unique. This was true for Jesus when He walked among us. It was true for Paul as He learned how to be all things to all people as shared in 1 Corinthians 9. And it is true for you and me today.

# Notes/Journal

Take some time to write down your thoughts and questions.
Write down Scriptures, what you've learned, and what you want
to learn more about.

This shows us how vital it is that we read Jesus's words when He was talking with those who were saved, those who were searching, those who were religious, and those who were not interested. There are different words and tones and outcomes each and every time.

Paul learned this. He did not know how to do it. He *learned* how to be all things for all mankind in order that some may be saved. For Paul, it was not defeat if a conversation did not end in salvation. For he understood that he was there to plant a seed or to water a seed previously planted by another. He learned how to engage with the weak and the strong, with the saved and the unsaved, with the single and the married, with the barbarian and the Jew. He learned these things by talking to many people in various opportunities over the years.

Today is the beginning of our learning what Paul learned as he followed the example set by Jesus Christ in the flesh.

So, where do we begin?

**Step One:** Study Paul's vision and technique.

**Step Two:** Create your vision.

# Notes/Journal

Take some time to write down your thoughts and questions.
Write down Scriptures, what you've learned, and what you want
to learn more about.

As you create your vision, I encourage you to create it as you are, where you are. Make a list of places you go. Consider who you tend to talk to at these places, what you tend to talk about with the people in these places. Sketch your normal existence on paper. See your daily encounters in front of you.

This list you have created is now your prayer list and your new life lesson. You're welcome.

I Corinthians 9 details what Paul learned as he created his vision. Spend time with Paul and see what he saw around him. Detail the personalities and the struggles he witnessed all around him—struggles of weakness and legalism, of worldly and upright, of those on the Rock and off the Rock.

See what Paul saw, and learn what Paul learned. For he learned that there is not one method that brings all mankind to Jesus. There is simply one Name to proclaim in the midst of living—Jesus.

As a group, share your vision, your list of people, and role-play some real-life encounters. You are the person on your list: think like this person, feel like this person. And listen to the words and the questions given to you by those in your group.

# Notes/Journal

Take some time to write down your thoughts and questions.
Write down Scriptures, what you've learned, and what you want
to learn more about.

# Homework

**Step One:** Develop the mentality of observation everywhere you go.

**Step Two:** As you develop this mentality, purpose to see each person's position on or off the Rock.

**Step Three:** Create an opportunity for dialogue every chance you get.

**Goal:** To seek out an opportunity to bring the conversation to your target Salvation Sentence. Make it natural and normal. Refrain from adding any detail or minimizing the power of Jesus in your life. If a question is asked, then respond in a way that will keep the focus centered around your Salvation Sentence.

**Remember:** If a responding question is not offered by your friend, family, etc., that is okay. Continue in conversation with your person. Engage in life and laughter with that person knowing that you planted a seed. Pray for the one who will water that seed. Pray for an opportunity to water that seed yourself. Pray for that person's salvation. And be present in their life as the person they know you to be. Be real. Be trusted as their person. Be you. Be Jesus in you. It's a good person to be!

# Homework

Who in your life is on the Rock? Who in your life is off the Rock? List their names here.

## On the Rock

## Off the Rock

# Memory Goal

Romans 10:13 ESV

"For 'everyone
who calls on the name of the Lord
will be saved.'"

# *Place Four* - In His Presence

## How do I lead them to proclaim the name of Jesus?

You've proclaimed Jesus through your Salvation Sentence. You've engaged in conversation with your person. You've responded to each question and statement through your target sentence. The Holy Spirit is evidently working in both your person's heart and yours. What do you do at this point? What do you say? Where do you go from here?

# Notes/Journal

Take some time to write down your thoughts and questions.
Write down Scriptures, what you've learned, and what you want
to learn more about.

All too often, it is at this point that we panic or overload our brain with the "right thing to say" which leads to self-dependency and often self-doubt.

May I encourage you to trust the Lord your God? Trust Him at this very moment in this very conversation with all your heart.

What does that mean? That means that the Holy Spirit has been working before this conversation with this person ever made it on your calendar. The seed of Jesus was planted before you. The watering has been taking place within this person's life by the Holy Spirit through outlets He controls. You are simply part of the working of the Holy Spirit in calling this lost soul to God through the love of Jesus Christ.

Consider the depth of this truth. The Holy Spirit has been working in this person's life. Furthermore, the Holy Spirit has been working in your life. Connect this truth deep within your heart. You are in this conversation because the Holy Spirit desires for you to be a part of this conversation.

This grand design is bigger than your level of knowledge of Scripture or "the right words." This grand design is about three things:

- Jesus Christ
- Jesus's love for this person
- Jesus in you

# Notes/Journal

Take some time to write down your thoughts and questions.
Write down Scriptures, what you've learned, and what you want
to learn more about.

When we bring these three things to the table, then the Holy Spirit can continue to do the work that He has been doing since the beginning of life—drawing His creation to God the Father through the life of God the Son. How gracious is He to entrust His creation to participate in the drawing of another to God by our personal experience of being drawn to God, by the Holy Spirit, and through the life of Jesus Christ.

I pray you see the beauty of this full circle. Let us not sidestep from the truth of Jesus and say things like:

- *This book changed my life.*
- *This study grew my faith.*
- *This church opened my eyes.*
- *This tangible thing did this momentary thing.*

It's about Jesus. Tangible items or locations are tools, yes, but they are not the eternal answer. Jesus is. In place of sidestepping to a tangible source, let us say simple truths such as these:

- *Jesus changed my life.*
- *I was this.*
- *Now I am this.*
- *And it all started when I accepted Jesus as my Lord.*

It's Jesus. Jesus is the way to Heaven. Jesus is the truth of your change. Jesus is the life you are living now. All because of Jesus's life and death and life eternal.

# Notes/Journal

Take some time to write down your thoughts and questions.
Write down Scriptures, what you've learned, and what you want
to learn more about.

Again, be careful not to extend time on the details of your "I was this" dialogue. Allow Jesus to be the sole content of your story.

### Jesus changed my life.

At this point, pause and pray within your heart that God will pinpoint what aspect of your story He wants you to share with this one person at this exact moment. Not all people need all of our story. When we share too much it becomes about us. It becomes about life on earth. We want it to always be about Jesus. Always about life eternal.

### I was _____.

If the Lord brings to memory a life moment or a sentence of your past that you do not often think about, then trust that He is using this piece to connect to the heart of the hearer sitting before you. This conversation is not about you. Remember that, friend. Trust the Lord with all your heart and with all your mind.

It is here that we may want to withdraw from remembering who we once were. To remember our past may sound painful to our ears, taste badly on our tongue. But, friend, remember that the Holy Spirit is in this conversation. This piece of your story that He desires to use is not who you are today. It is a piece of history. It is not you. Allow the Holy Spirit to use it.

# Notes/Journal

Take some time to write down your thoughts and questions.
Write down Scriptures, what you've learned, and what you want
to learn more about.

*Now I am _____.*

I do not know how to put this segment in words beyond a smile of awe! This is when we simply sit in admiration of the transformation only God could do. Selah.

Will you sit with me as I write what Jesus did for me? Then will you sit and write what Jesus did for you? Our words will be similar, for Jesus did the same thing for each of us.

*Jesus took my sin of _____ and wore it as if it were His own. Just that thought brings tears to my eyes. To think that He was willing to identify Himself as a _____ in public humiliation on a cross before God and before His accusers—it's too much to bear. Even still, He conquered it by dying and burying it. He disallowed it to be my identity any longer. And then He rose again bringing life to all who call upon His name. I called on His name. How could I not? Jesus did that for me, and I want to live free from that sin. I want to walk in His identity of love and forgiveness and newness. So I called upon Jesus. I thanked Him for taking my sin, for dying for my sin. I asked Him to forgive me. And He did. I know He did because . . . here I am, somehow living in love and forgiveness and newness. I am no longer known as one who _____. I am now in love with Jesus.*

# Notes/Journal

Take some time to write down your thoughts and questions. Write down Scriptures, what you've learned, and what you want to learn more about.

Just by setting yourself at the foot of the cross and standing yourself before the Throne of God, you can share both Jesus's story of redemption and Jesus's story in you at the same time. Simple and powerful and real.

**And it all started when I accepted Jesus as my Lord.**

From here, we want to offer Jesus's call to salvation to the hearer. I encourage you to continue in your story.

*I remember hearing how simply Jesus offers His gift of salvation. Just as much as this is Jesus's story in me, it's Jesus's story in everyone who believes in who He is as the eternal Son of God. Anyone who believes that Jesus died and rose again is saved. It wasn't my works or performance or getting my life in order. . . . It was believing in Jesus. I believed in Him, and He changed my life. May I say, Jesus wore your sin, too. He died for your sin and conquered it just as He did mine.*

**There are two questions to ask at this point:**

- *Do you believe that Jesus is the Son of God?*

- *Do you want to call on Jesus to be your Lord today?*

# Notes/Journal

Take some time to write down your thoughts and questions.
Write down Scriptures, what you've learned, and what you want
to learn more about.

**If your hearer says *YES* . . .**

Be real with your response. Smile. Tear up. Rejoice. And introduce them to the One who knows them so fully! At this point Romans 10 is a miraculous passage to refer to. If there is a Bible (or YouVersion app) near you, open to Romans 10. Allow verses 9 and 10 to take the lead. You will read:

> *Because, if you confess with your mouth*
> *that Jesus is Lord*
> *and believe in your heart*
> *that God raised him from the dead,*
> *you will be saved.*
> *For with the heart one believes and is justified,*
> *and with the mouth one confesses and is saved.*
> *For "everyone who calls on the name of the Lord*
> *will be saved."*
> **Romans 10:9–10, 13**

Bring emphasis to the words *confess with your mouth that Jesus is Lord*. There is not an exact salvation prayer, but there are salvation words, and there is a Hearer ready to listen!

The Hearer is God. The words are spoken from the heart of the new believer, words of faith believing that God raised Jesus from the dead, words declaring that they believe that Jesus is Lord.

# Notes/Journal

Take some time to write down your thoughts and questions. Write down Scriptures, what you've learned, and what you want to learn more about.

Rejoice with this new believer as they just entered an eternal relationship with God, fully loved and fully forgiven. How miraculous is this truth!

**If your hearer says *NO* ...**

Encourage this hearer to ponder the love of Jesus in their own timing. Ask them if they would consider simply thinking about it. Don't force an answer to that request. Simply lay that out for them.

Conversation may feel a tad awkward at this moment. That is okay. Be comfortable with silence. Don't try to fix it or belittle the situation. Allow them the opportunity to switch gears. When they do, engage. Be present. Be responsive. Be you. Be Jesus in you. Remember, that's a good thing to be.

Remind yourself that you watered a beautiful seed planted by the Holy Spirit. Trust the Lord, fully! Do not lean on your understanding of the situation. Trust that the Spirit understands the heart of the hearer. And pray with the Spirit over this soul.

Remember this: The amazing truth of the love of Jesus is that He died for our sins when we were sinners, living in our sin, completely unaware of our choice to believe. Basically, whether we believe it or not, our sins were paid for. How do we comprehend such love?

# Notes/Journal

Take some time to write down your thoughts and questions.
Write down Scriptures, what you've learned, and what you want
to learn more about.

- When we believe, we live a life inseparable of the love of God. Our eternal relationship with God (full of love and forgiveness and all things new) begins today. We get to live in this physical life wrapped in His love and forgiveness until the day we die and meet our Savior and our God, face-to-face.

- When we do not believe, we perish in eternal separation from God. We continue in a physical life on earth void of His love and forgiveness. We die destined to an eternal separation from God in Heaven, to an eternity in Hell.

Our decision to believe in Jesus determines our life today, and it destines our life eternally.

# Notes/Journal

Take some time to write down your thoughts and questions.
Write down Scriptures, what you've learned, and what you want
to learn more about.

# Homework

It's time to practice.

Rehearse Jesus's full story as you insert your story in a little at a time. See what that looks like. You may want to write it out to see how God can use little pieces of your story within the big story of Jesus's love on the cross, in the tomb, and risen again. Remember to keep the emphasis on Jesus, always.

Engage in conversation during workshop times. Take turns sharing the story of Jesus with one another. Receive a question from your hearer to practice inserting a piece of your story into Jesus's story. Continue this process until one of you reaches the call to salvation. Then pray words of salvation together.

Please do not rush to this point. Knowing how the Holy Spirit can use you and your story is fundamental to leading others to Jesus. Learn how to listen to the prompting of the Holy Spirit during these practice sessions.

Remember, you are practicing these conversations before the Throne with others who are on the Rock. If you get stuck, talk to God together. Pray for words from the One you desire to proclaim. Then try again, boldly.

# Homework

Simple truths and Scriptures
that sound like my heart, my voice.

| Simple Truths | Scriptures |
|---|---|
|  |  |
|  |  |
|  |  |
|  |  |
|  |  |

# Homework

## Jesus's Story in Your Own Words

Take some time to write out what Jesus did
in His death, burial, and resurrection.

_____

_____

_____

_____

_____

_____

_____

_____

_____

_____

_____

_____

_____

_____

# Memory Goal

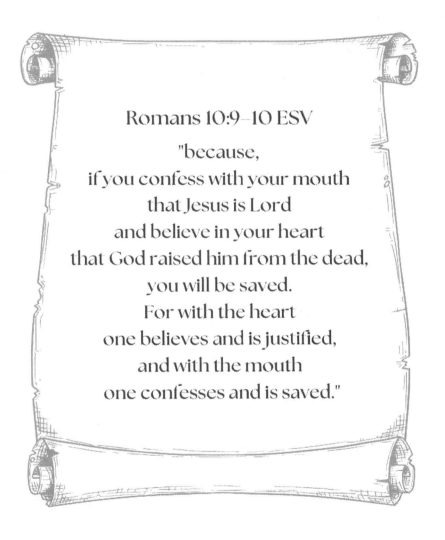

Romans 10:9–10 ESV

"because,
if you confess with your mouth
that Jesus is Lord
and believe in your heart
that God raised him from the dead,
you will be saved.
For with the heart
one believes and is justified,
and with the mouth
one confesses and is saved."

# In Closing

Thank you for investing in your relationship with your Lord and Savior Jesus Christ. May you press on in full confidence of who you are, knowing that you are God's. And as God's, you are always and forever At the Cross, Before the Throne, On the Rock, and In His Presence.

May you live your life with these truths wrapped around your day, your steps, and your heart. I pray that those on the Rock around you will grow in their love for Jesus Christ simply by worshiping Jesus alongside your joy in Him. And I pray that those who are off the Rock will come and see what it is that is different within you.

May the name and the salvation of Jesus Christ multiply in you and through you simply by being you, in love with the love of God that is found in Christ Jesus our Lord.

When you are ready for more Scripture studies to do with the Lord, with friends, or with the women of your church, join **Women Inseparable** in our other studies and social platforms shared below.

## In His Likeness

To identify the character of man we must first identify the character of God, Jesus, and the Holy Spirit. May we grow in our ability to see others and ourselves In His Likeness!

## In the Light

The power and presence of Light is seen throughout Scripture. During this 9-week Scripture study, may our eyes see what it looks like to walk and live In The Light—as we are, where we are.

## Who Holds Forgiveness?

Forgiveness stirs up multiple emotions within our souls. May we sit in the Master's hand to see what forgiveness looks like from that viewpoint.

## But God!

Everyone has a story. May we be open to seeing our story as a light for His glory. Learn how to listen to your story and to share it with someone in need.

## Jesus & Me Today

Scripture declares, "Jesus is coming again." But what does that truth look like in our daily lives? Learn how to live today as you earnestly wait for tomorrow.

## Prayer & Fasting

A 2-part, 20-week study that will grow your prayer life and your fasting life into what God desires it to be—a rich, ongoing conversation between God's heart and yours.

# About Women Inseparable

We are women who stand together on the promise of Jesus Christ's love that He displayed on the cross, sealed in the grave, and eternally proclaimed in His resurrection!

As followers of Jesus, we are Inseparable of Christ's love despite our various journeys of life, our joys, our pains, our society, our culture, our location, or the physical distance between us. And in His love, we stand together in Prayer, Scripture, and Girl Time, proudly declaring that we are **Women Inseparable.**

*Who shall separate us from the love of Christ?*
*Shall tribulation, or distress, or persecution,*
*or famine, or nakedness, or danger, or sword?*
*As it is written,*
*"For your sake we are being killed all the day long;*
*we are regarded as sheep to be slaughtered."*
*No, in all these things we are more than conquerors*
*through him who loved us.*
*For I am sure that neither death nor life,*
*nor angels nor rulers,*
*nor things present nor things to come,*
*nor powers, nor height nor depth,*
*nor anything else in all creation,*
*will be able to separate us from the love of God*
*in Christ Jesus our Lord.*
***Romans 8:35–39 ESV***

# About the Author

## Jaclyn Palmer

Author, Speaker, Bible Teacher

God's grace was evident in Jaclyn's life from an early age, allowing her to grow up in the Christian faith. She personally came to faith in Jesus Christ at a young age. She now ministers to local churches and women's ministries with a heart of compassion and the unique ability to bring joy into the lives of the most hurting people.

Jaclyn is the founder of **Women Inseparable**. She is a women's Bible teacher, speaker, and author of *The Beautiful Reward* and *Stand in Truth*.

She embraces teaching Scripture and writing studies that offer a sweet relationship with Jesus Christ. With a forty-year relationship with Jesus and a passionate love for the Word of God, Jaclyn is a voice for simple truths. She lives in Idaho with her husband and son.

To learn more, come and join Jaclyn and the amazing community of women on womeninseparable.com.

## HOW TO CONTACT US:

Email us at:
inseparableministriesinc@gmail.com

Write us at:
Inseparable Ministries Publishing
1200 N Main Street
Meridian, Idaho 83680

WOMENINSEPARABLE.COM

Made in the USA
Columbia, SC
08 June 2023

17839863R00043